the QUOTABLE WINSTON CHURCHILL

the
QUOTABLE
WINSTON
CHURCHILL

Edited by Richard J. Mahoney with Shera Dalin

Illustrated by Dan Martin

**WINSTON
CHURCHILL**
MEMORIAL AND LIBRARY

The Quotable Winston Churchill is published in cooperation with
the Winston Churchill Memorial and Library in Fulton, Missouri.
Copyright 2005.

Edited by Richard J. Mahoney with Shera Dalin
Art Director: Janet Muhm, St. Louis, Missouri

Printed in the United States

ISBN 0-9767843-0-0

CONTENTS

◆ ◆ ◆ ◆ ◆

A REMEMBRANCE
by Margaret Thatcher

◆ ◆ ◆ ◆ ◆

To provide an auspicious beginning to this collection, we asked Margaret Thatcher, Great Britain's prime minister from 1979 to 1990, for her favorite quote from Winston Churchill. There are a number that she is particularly fond of, but one which she used often in discussing Britain's friendship with the United States. The quote comes from Churchill's famous "Iron Curtain" speech.

Addressing his American audience, he said:

> "If all the British moral and material forces and convictions are joined with your own in fraternal association, the highroads of the future will be clear not only for us, but for all, not only for our time, but for a century to come."

Fifty years later, Lady Thatcher was invited to Westminster College in Fulton, Missouri, to mark the anniversary of Churchill's speech and to deliver her own warnings on the challenges that Britain and America faced in the future. Lady Thatcher sounded a strong alarm against the revival of a Russian foreign policy that would be less friendly to the United States, and she decried the proliferation of weapons of mass destruction in the hands of "rogue states," which she called the "single most awesome threat of modern times."

She remarked in that address:

"Like my uniquely distinguished predecessor, I too may be accused of alarmism in pointing to new dangers to which present institutions–and attitudes–are proving unequal. But, also like him, I have every confidence in the resources and the values of the Western civilisation we are defending."

INTRODUCTION

◆ ◆ ◆ ◆ ◆

The Winston Churchill Memorial and Library was dedicated in 1969 in recognition of the famous speech by Churchill at Fulton, Missouri, on March 5, 1946, entitled "The Sinews of Peace." It became known as "The Iron Curtain Speech," his most important post-World War II address, in which he warned of the rise of Soviet domination of Eastern Europe long before most Western leaders chose to consider the threat.

The museum was a remarkable facility, capturing many images of Churchill recognizable to people who shared his times. In 2003, it was decided to renovate the museum to make Churchill more accessible to a new generation and to be appreciated by them—to focus on his leadership role for the ages.

I was asked to select from his thousands of quotations and pick just those few hundred that would be featured in an exhibit called "The Wit and Wisdom Room."

It was a daunting task.

A number of books had been written using the title or allusions to the subject of the wit and wisdom of Winston Churchill. His wise statements fill the dozens of books written about his life and leadership. Many of the collections, however, were designed for English audiences. They contained references that Americans would sometimes not fully understand because of the context of the times in which they were uttered. Therefore, they sometimes no longer seemed particularly "witty." Other collections were created to be "complete"– worthy and helpful selections, but not designed to delight and inspire Americans who perhaps knew something of Churchill–but were not of his time and, thus, unable to fully appreciate the nuances of his lines. The quotations for the new Wit and Wisdom Room at the museum are selected to be appreciated on their own–for insights they provide. They portray Churchill for our times and all times–a glimpse of a master of the English language.

It would be easy to focus only on his acerbic wit: Putting down Lady Astor in the House of Commons with the well-known exchange, "Winston, if I were your wife, I'd put poison in your coffee."

"Nancy," Churchill replied, "if I were your husband, I would drink it."

But there were many more statements which displayed a compassion, phrasing, and decency which too often go unquoted in the anthologies: "A nation without a conscience is a nation without a soul. A nation without a soul is a nation that cannot live." Or of Franklin Roosevelt: "He died on the wings of victory, but he saw them and heard them beating."

This collection is grouped in several categories as shown in the index. Like those of many famous people, the sayings of Churchill are often difficult to trace to precise origins. Additionally, when he found a phrase he particularly liked he used it, slightly revised, on more than one occasion. For example, the German proverb "The trees do not grow to the sky" appears more than a dozen times in citations of Churchill's works. Indeed, proverbs were a rich source for Churchill. It is estimated that he used some, 3,300 proverbial references in his published corpus of 37,000 pages.

Some of the quotations cited in this book may be merely apocryphal—but not many. Most have been verified by multiple sources.

With these few reservations, I present what I think are words that can be understood and appreciated by all who cherish the English language and the man who mobilized it for war and peace.

Richard J. Mahoney
St. Louis, Missouri
2005

THE WIT OF CHURCHILL

◆ ◆ ◆ ◆ ◆

"Churchill will live if only in his witticisms. And these will be the stock of conversation in all countries for a long time to come. They are as much a revelation of character as anything he said or did—as much, also, of an influence among men. In wartime they passed by word of mouth all over the world wherever men were struggling with the aggressor and planning a new life in liberty. They lightened the burdens of the dispirited and were quoted as the words of a champion."

> – Herbert Elliston, late editor of The Washington Post

"It used to be one of the pleasures of my life to watch him preparing to make a joke at a public meeting. One always knew it was coming. His own laughter began somewhere in the region of his feet. Then a leg would twitch; the bubble of mirth was slowly rising through the body. The stomach would swell; a shoulder, heave. By this time the audience would be convulsed, although it had no idea what the joke was going to be."

> – Hugh Massingham, political writer, The Sunday Telegraph

"Perhaps the most endearing thing about him in private talk, in cabinet, in the House of Commons, was his puckish humour, his tremendous sense of fun, and the quick alternation between grave and gay."

– Harold Macmillan, Conservative member of Parliament; Prime Minister, 1957-1963

"There are the looks magnanimous, contemptuous, indifferent, very bored, mischievous, somber, despairing, arrogant. Only one look is missing: the look apologetic. When he gets up to go–the vitality of the House goes with him. It subsides like a reception after the champagne is finished."

– Woodrow Wyatt, Labour member of Parliament

"When I get to heaven, I mean to spend a considerable
portion of my first million years in painting, and so,
get to the bottom of the subject."

Maxims

◆ ◆ ◆ ◆ ◆

"In my belief you cannot deal with the most serious things in the world unless you also understand the most amusing."

"A nation without a conscience is a nation without a soul. A nation without a soul is a nation that cannot live."

– Speech to the RAF Benevolent Fund, 1951

On decisive leadership:

"One cannot leap a chasm in two jumps."

"I am reminded of the remark of the witty Irishman who said: 'There are a terrible lot of lies going about the world, and the worst of it is that about half of them are true.'"

– South Africa, 1906

"Change is the master key. A man can wear out a particular part of his mind by continually using it and tiring it, just in the same way as he can wear out the elbows of his coat."

Advice to his literary assistant John Wheldon, whose attention to detail was delaying progress:
"Do not let the better be the enemy of the good."

"It is wonderful how well men can keep secrets they have not been told."

"We are happier in many ways when we are old than when we are young. The young sow wild oats; the old grow sage."

"What most people call bad judgment is judgment which is different than theirs."

"The maxim: 'Nothing avails but perfection' may be
spelt shorter: 'p-a-r-a-l-y-s-i-s.'"

> – *The Second World War, Volume IV*

"Of this I am quite sure: That if we open a quarrel
between the past and the present, we shall find
we have lost the future."

"The farthest backward you can look, the farther forward
you can see."

"You must look at the facts because they look at you."

> – *1925*

"It is a mistake to look too far ahead. Only one link in the
chain of destiny can be handled at a time."

To a waiter:

  "Pray take away this pudding–it has no theme."

"Golf is like chasing a quinine pill around a pasture."

"Golf is a game whose aim is to hit a very small ball into an even smaller hole, with weapons singularly ill designed for the purpose."

"It is a very fine thing to refuse an invitation, but it is a good thing to wait until you get it first."

On the reaction of the press to liberal support for Irish home rule:

"The Times is speechless, and takes three columns to express its speechlessness."

During an argument with his cousin Lord Londonderry, who asked if Churchill had read his latest book Ourselves and Germany:

"No. I only read for pleasure or profit."

"Writing a book was an adventure. To begin with, it was a toy, an amusement; then it became a mistress, and then a master, and then a tyrant."

– London, 1949

"Writing a book is not unlike building a house or planning a battle or painting a picture. The foundations have to be laid, the data assembled, and the premises must bear the weight of their conclusions. Ornaments or refinement may then be added."

– *My Early Life: A Roving Commission*

On government power over broadcasting during wartime:

"I think we should have to retain a certain amount of power in selection of the music. Very spirited renderings of *Deutschland Über Alles* would hardly be permissible."

On whether a pacifist should be excluded from an orchestra:

"I see no reason to suppose that the holding of pacifist views would make him play flat."

"Youth is for freedom and reform, maturity for judicious compromise, and old age for stability and repose."

Upon receiving an honorary degree from the University of Miami in Florida, one of 20 such honors he received:

"I am surprised that in my later life I should have become so experienced in taking degrees when as a schoolboy I was so bad at passing examinations. In fact, one might almost say that no one ever passed so few examinations and received so many degrees."

"Large views always triumph over small ideas."

On the Verandah Grill of the Queen Mary in New York Harbor in 1952:

"The television has come to take its place in the world. As a rather old-fashioned person, I have not been one of its principal champions, but I don't think it needs any champion. I think it can make its own way, and I think it's a wonderful thing indeed to think that every expression on my face at this moment may be viewed by millions of people throughout the United States. I hope that the raw material is as good as the methods of distribution."

"The truth is uncontrovertible. Panic may resent it; ignorance may deride it; malice may destroy it; but there it is."

"The essence of American journalism is vulgarity divested of truth."

In response to a BBC spokesman, noting that the network had a duty to air both sides of the debate on Christianity versus atheism:

"I suppose then that if there had been the same devices at the time of Christ, the BBC would have given equal time to Judas and Jesus."

"I always avoid prophesying beforehand because it is much better policy to prophesy after the event has already taken place."

"The spectacle of a number of middle-aged gentlemen who are my political opponents being in a state of uproar and fury is really quite exhilarating to me."

"I cannot pretend to feel impartial about colours. I rejoice with the brilliant ones and am genuinely sorry for the poor browns."

– Painting as a Pastime

"When I get to heaven, I mean to spend a considerable portion of my first million years in painting, and so get to the bottom of the subject."

– Painting as a Pastime

"Let us therefore brace ourselves to our duties, and so bear ourselves that, if the British Empire and its Commonwealth last for a thousand years, men will still say: 'This was their finest hour.'"

– House of Commons, 1940

"If we look back on our past life, we shall see that one of its most usual experiences is that we have been helped by our mistakes and injured by our most sagacious decisions."

"It is always, I think, true to say that one of the main foundations of the British sense of humour is understatement."

– House of Commons, July 27, 1950

"Remember the story of the Spanish prisoner. For many years he was confined in a dungeon. One day it occurred to him to push the door of his cell. It was open, and it had never been locked."

Referring to being shot at in 1897 with the Malakand Field Force in India:

"Nothing in life is as exhilarating as to be shot at without result."

From a friend: "Winston, how wonderfully your new grandson resembles you!"

Churchill: "All babies look like me. But then I look like all babies."

"Never give in! Never give in! Never, never, never, never—
in nothing great and small—large and petty. Never give in
except to convictions of honour and good sense."

– Harrow School, 1941

"Although prepared for martyrdom, I prefer that it
shall be postponed."

On death:

"We make too much of it. All religions do.
Of course, I may alter my views."

"Never in the field of human conflict was so much
owed by so many to so few."

– House of Commons, August 20, 1940

As he gazed into a fire shortly before his death:

"I know what it's like to be a log: reluctant to be consumed
but yielding in the end to persuasion."

VICES

"Always remember Clemmie, that I have taken more out of alcohol than alcohol has taken out of me."

VICES
◆ ◆ ◆ ◆ ◆

"Winston, you are drunk, and what's more, you are disgustingly drunk," accused Liverpool Labourite member Bessie Braddock one evening in the House of Commons.

"And might I say, Mrs. Braddock," Churchill replied, "you are ugly and what's more, disgustingly ugly. But tomorrow, I shall be sober."

✻

"Prof, if all the wine and spirits that I have drunk in a lifetime was poured into this salon, do you think it would reach the ceiling?" Churchill once asked physicist and science advisor Lord Cherwell.

Cherwell made some calculations on his slide rule and pronounced: "Prime Minister, if all the alcohol you have consumed in your life were to occupy this room, I estimate that it would only reach the level of your eye."

A dismayed Churchill commented, "As I gaze at the ceiling and contemplate my 75 years, my only thought is—how much left to do and how little time to do it."

"When I was a young subaltern in the South Africa campaign, the water was not fit to drink. To make it palatable, we had to add whiskey. By diligent effort I learned to like it".

(Churchill's preferred whiskey was said to be Johnnie Walker Red Label, and he was a friend of the distillery's one-time leader Alexander Walker.)

Commenting to his wife, Clementine:

"Always remember, Clemmie, that I have taken more out of alcohol than alcohol has taken out of me."

"A single glass of champagne imparts a feeling of exhilaration. The nerves are braced; the imagination is agreeably stirred; the wits become more nimble. A bottle produces a contrary effect. Excess causes a comotosed insensibility. So it is with war; and the quality of both is best discovered by sipping."

– *The Story of the Malakand Field Force*

On brandy:

"I neither want it, nor need it, but I think it pretty hazardous to interfere with the ineradicable habit of a lifetime."

"Good cognac is like a woman. Do not assault it; coddle and warm it in your hands before you sip it."

"When I was younger I made it a rule never to take strong drink before lunch. It is now my rule never to do so before breakfast."

To the Iraqi ambassador after a state banquet at 10 Downing Street:

"Ambassador, why don't you come back to my study for a nightcap?"

"Mr. Churchill," he replied, "I can't. I'm a Muslim."

"What? You don't drink? Good God. I mean Jesus Christ...I mean Allah!"

While attending a reception during a speaking tour in Canada, a Methodist minister refused a glass of sherry offered by a waitress, saying "Young lady, I'd rather commit adultery than take an intoxicating beverage."

Churchill hailed the server: "Come back lassie. I didn't know we had a choice."

Responding to a temperance group's request that he forego christening a ship with a bottle of champagne:

"The hallowed custom of the Royal Navy is indeed a splendid example of temperance. The ship takes its first sip of wine and then proceeds on water ever after."

"All the years that I have been in the House of Commons I have always said to myself one thing: 'Do not interrupt,' and I have never been able to keep to that resolution."

Upon learning that his life had been threatened before a lecture in New York City, he gave his agent immediate instructions:

"Please fetch me a bottle of champagne."

"I had better go ahead and make plans against these plots," his agent responded.

"First things first. Get the champagne," said Churchill, whose contract required that he be given a bottle before each engagement.

(Churchill was fond of Pol Roget Champagne. The firm still produces a commemorative Churchill champagne.)

"Tobacco is bad for love; but old age is worse."

"Personally I am always ready to learn, although I do not always like being taught."

During a raucous family meal, as related by daughter
Sarah Churchill:

"Randolph, do stop interrupting me while I'm
interrupting you!"

"I am a sporting man. I always like to give trains and
aeroplanes a fair chance of getting away."

"Unpunctuality is a vile habit, and all my life I have tried to
break myself of it."

At a dinner for the Prince of Wales, later Edward VII:

"I realized that I must be on my best behaviour–
punctual, subdued, reserved–in short, display all the
qualities with which I am least endowed."

– 1896

"Never trust a man who has not a single redeeming vice."

While visiting a parachute factory Churchill absentmindedly reached for a cigar, prompting the fire officer to admonish him not to smoke:

"Oh, don't worry, dear boy," Churchill responded.
"I don't inhale."

"Smoking cigars is like falling in love. First you are attracted to its shape; you stay with it for its flavor; and you must always remember never, never, let the flame go out."

"Vanity! The vice that promotes so many virtues."

When advised of the risk of contracting an infection while visiting the Kasbah before a meeting with U.S. President Franklin Roosevelt Churchill replied:

"Ah ha! So you think there's life in the old dog yet, do you? I assure you, my friends, that even if I were to go to the Kasbah and contract the disease which you have in mind, I should be most unlikely to communicate it to the president."

On religion:

"My various readings…led me to ask myself questions about religion. Hitherto, I had dutifully accepted everything I had been told. I had always had to go once a week to Church. All this was very good. I accumulated in those years so fine a surplus in the Bank of Observance that I have been drawing confidently upon it ever since. Weddings, christenings, and funerals have brought in a steady annual income, and I have never made too close enquiries about the state of my account. It might well even be that I should find an overdraft."

– My Early Life

When asked, as a young boy, how many demerits he had received at school that day, he replied, "Nine."

"Nine seems even too much for you, Winston," the teacher replied.

"The word I used was *nein*, German for 'no.'" he explained.

Before Churchill's arrival at the Plaza Hotel in New York, the manager phoned the British embassy in Washington, D.C. to seek information about the prime minister's preferences. In the middle of his call, a new but familiar voice inquired "Yes?"

"I am the director of the Plaza Hotel inquiring about Mr. Churchill's tastes–"

"Mr. Churchill," interrupted the famously resonant voice, "is a man of simple tastes–easily satisfied with the best."

❧

"If this is a world of vice and woe, I'll take the vice, and you can have the woe."

GOVERNMENT & ECONOMIES

"Some see private enterprise as a predatory animal
to be shot, others look on it as a cow to be milked,
but a few see it as a sturdy horse pulling a wagon."

Government & Economies
♦ ♦ ♦ ♦ ♦

"Many forms of government have been tried and will be tried in this world of sin and woe. No one pretends that Democracy is perfect or all-wise. Indeed, it has been said that Democracy is the worst form of government, except all those other forms that have been tried from time to time."

— House of Commons

Churchill often used the same imagery:

"The best argument against Democracy is a five-minute conversation with the average voter. No one pretends that Democracy is perfect or all-wise. Indeed it has been said that Democracy is the worst form of government, except all those other forms that have been tried from time to time"

Prior to his failed campaign for a seat in Parliament, Churchill had his appendix removed.

"In the twinkling of an eye I found myself without an office, without a seat, without a party, and without an appendix."

— *Thoughts and Adventures*

Describing a parliamentary candidate:
"He is asked to stand, he wants to sit, he is expected to lie."

While canvassing for votes in 1900, Churchill encountered some opposition.

"Vote for you?" one citizen exclaimed. "Why I'd rather vote for the Devil!"

"I understand," Churchill answered. "But in case your friend is not running, may I count on your support?"

"Some see private enterprise as a predatory animal to be shot, others look on it as a cow to be milked, but a few see it as a sturdy horse pulling a wagon."

"The practice of Parliament must be judged by quality, not quantity. You cannot judge the passing of laws by Parliament as you would judge the output of an efficient Chicago bacon factory."

In opposing peace at any price:

"Look at the Swiss! They have enjoyed peace for centuries. And what have they produced? The cuckoo clock!"

– 1938

On the Labour Government:

"One can quite easily see that if they have their way they will reduce this powerful country to one vast soup kitchen."

– London, 1929

During budget preparations, he asked his advisors to explain certain figures:

"They sent for a little man from the basement, who in words of one syllable told me exactly what those figures meant. I thanked him. He went back to his basement and was never seen again.

"The higher mind has no need to concern itself with the meticulous regimentation of figures."

– 1924

"Lord Jowitt has brought disgrace to the name of rat."

– 1923

(In English politics, "to rat" was to change political parties.)

Commenting on a Conservative member running as a Liberal in a special election:

"The only instance of a rat swimming towards
a sinking ship."

– 1923

Having left the Conservative party to join the Liberals and then to rejoin the Conservatives:

"Anyone can rat, but it takes a certain amount of ingenuity
to re-rat."

– 1931

"The small fry of the Tory Party splashing actively about in their Tory puddles…fall back on their dukes. These unfortunate individuals who ought to lead quiet, delicate, sheltered lives, far from the maddening crowd's ignoble strife have been dragged into the football scrimmage, and they have got rather mauled in the process…. Do not be too hard on them. It is poor sport…almost like teasing goldfish. These ornamental creatures blunder on every hook they see, and there is no sport whatever in trying to catch them. It would be barbarous to leave them gasping upon the bank of public ridicule, upon which they have landed themselves. Let us put them back gently, tenderly in their fountains; and if a few bright gold scales have rubbed off in what the Prime Minister calls the variegated handling they have received, they will soon get over it. They have got plenty more."

– as reported in *The Times of London* in 1909

❦

"Some men change their party for the sake of their principles; others change their principles for the sake of their party."

– 1906

❦

"Politics is like waking up in the morning. You never know whose head you'll find on the pillow."

Responding to the suggestion of friend, journalist and politician Leo Amery that Churchill might break away from the Conservative Party when it moved back to tariffs and protectionism:

"I shall stick to you with all the loyalty of a leech."

Before a joint session of the U.S. Congress:

"I cannot help reflecting that if my father had been American and my mother British, instead of the other way around, I might have got here on my own.

He went on: "In that case, this would not have been the first time you would have heard my voice. I should not have needed any invitation, but if I had, it is hardly likely that it would have been unanimous. I owe my advancement entirely to the House of Commons, whose servant I am. In my country, as in yours, public men are proud to be the servants of the state and would be ashamed to be its masters. On any day, if they thought the people wanted it, the House of Commons could by a simple vote remove me from my office. But I am not worrying about it at all."

– 1941

On construction of the Desert Railway in Sudan:

"From the growing workshops at Wadi Halfa, the continued clatter and clang of hammers and the black smoke of manufacture rose to the African sky. The malodorous incense of civilization was offered to the startled gods of Egypt."

– The River War

"There is a poetic justice in the fact that the most mischievous mouth in wartime has become in peace the most remarkable administrative failure."

Blackpool, 1946

"Democracy is not based on violence or terrorism, but on reason, on fair play, on freedom, on respecting the rights of other people. Democracy is no harlot to be picked up in the street by a man with a Tommy gun. I trust the people, the mass of the people, in almost any country, but I like to make sure that it is the people and not a gang of bandits who think that, by violence, they can overturn the constituted authority."

On civil servants:

"No longer servants, no longer civil."

"I am a child of the House of Commons. I was brought up in my father's house to believe in Democracy. 'Trust the people' was his message."

– U.S. Congress, 1941

"Some people's idea of free speech is that they are free to say what they like but if anyone says anything back, that is an outrage."

"If you destroy a free market, you create a black market."

– 1949

"The idea that a nation can tax itself into prosperity is one of the cruelest delusions which has ever befuddled the human mind."

"I have always felt that a politician is to be judged by the animosities he excites among his opponents."

"Expenditure always is popular; the only unpopular part about it is the raising of the money to pay the expenditure."

– House of Commons, 1901

On unemployment:

"We must try to seek the remedies of the disease, not merely the remedies for the symptoms."

"Hatred plays the same part in government as acid in chemistry."

– *Thoughts and Adventures*

"The electors, based on universal suffrage, may do what they like, and afterwards they have to like what they do."

– Blackpool, 1946

As his nurse removed a bed pan from his room, she heard him chuckling:

"I don't see anything funny about taking out a bed pan," she said.

"It's the first time that a motion [movement] of mine has been carried out since the Labour Government came in."

– 1946

On medicine:

"The only way to swallow a bitter mixture is to take it in a single gulp."

"Dictators ride to and fro upon tigers from which they dare not dismount. And the tigers are getting hungry."

– "Navy and National Defence Loan" speech, 1935

"The United States is like a gigantic boiler.
Once the fire is lit under it, there is no limit to the power
it can generate."

Nations

◆ ◆ ◆ ◆ ◆

"There have been many occasions when a powerful state has wished to raise great armies, and with money and time and discipline and loyalty, that can be accomplished. Nevertheless the rate at which the small American Army of only a few hundred thousand men, not long before the war, created the mighty force of millions of soldiers, is a wonder in military history."

– Pentagon 1946

꽃

Speaking to Mrs. Ogden Reid, an American who believed that the people of India had been oppressed by the British:

"Before we proceed further, let us get one thing clear. Are we talking about the brown Indians in India, who have multiplied alarmingly under the benevolent British rule, or are we speaking of the red Indians in America who, I understand, are almost extinct?"

– at a White House lunch given by President Franklin D. Roosevelt, 1943

"France, though armed to the teeth, is pacifist to the core."

– 1932

"The U.N. was set up not to get us to heaven but only to save us from hell."

"The proud German army has, by its sudden collapse, sudden crumbling and breaking up once again proved the truth of the saying. 'The Hun is always either at your throat or your feet.'"

– U.S. Congress, 1943

"I cannot forecast to you the action of Russia. It is a riddle wrapped in a mystery inside an enigma. But perhaps there is a key; that key is Russian national interest."

– 1939

"Not only the British empire and the United States, but the greater part of Europe, have a lively interest in China. China, as the years pass, is being eaten by Japan like an artichoke–leaf by leaf."

– 1936

"Japan's policy is to make hell while the sun shines."

"India is an abstraction…. India is no more a political personality than Europe. India is a geographical term. It is no more a united nation than the equator."

– Royal Albert Hall, London, 1931

Upon telling the Irish prime minister that the situation in the United Kingdom was "serious but not hopeless," the Irishman responded that the situation in his nation was "hopeless but not serious."

"I see no reason why there should not ultimately arise the United States of Europe."

– the Hague, 1946

"Upon Britain fell the proud but awful responsibility of keeping the flag of freedom flying in the Old World till the forces of the New World arrived."

– Brussels, 1945

"There are no people in the world who are so slow to develop hostile feelings against a foreign country as the Americans, and there are no people who, once estranged, are more difficult to win back. The American eagle sits on his perch, a large strong bird with formidable beak and claws. There he sits motionless and Mr. Gromyko [Soviet delegate to the United Nations] is sent day after day to prod him with a sharp-pointed stick–now his neck, now under his wings, now his tail feathers. All the time the eagle keeps quite still But it would be a great mistake to suppose that nothing is going on inside the breast of the eagle."

"The United States is like a gigantic boiler. Once the fire is lit under it, there is no limit to the power it can generate."

"We must also never allow the growing sense of unity and brotherhood between the United Kingdom and the United States and throughout the English-speaking world to be injured or retarded."

– House of Commons, 1955

"The British Empire and the United States will have to be somewhat mixed up together in some of their affairs for mutual and general advantage. For my own part, looking out for the future, I do not view the process with any misgivings. I could not stop it if I wished; no one can stop it. Like the Mississippi, it just keeps rolling along. Let it roll. Let it roll in full flood, inexorable, irresistible, benignant, to broader lands and better days."

– House of Commons, 1940

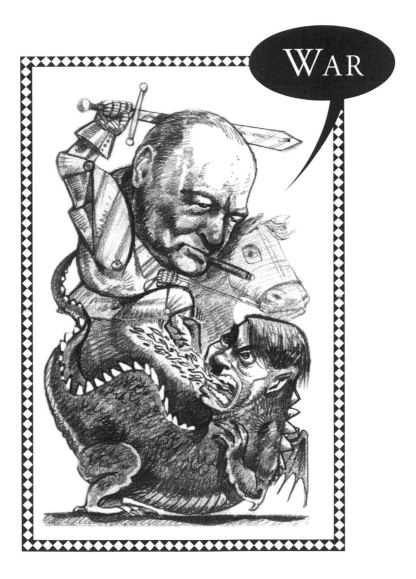

WAR

"War attracts me and fascinates my mind with its tremendous situations. What vile and wicked folly and barbarism it all is."

On the prospect of the outcome if a modern version of England's patron saint, George, had to slay a dragon and rescue a maiden in distress:

"St. George would arrive in Cappadocia accompanied, not by a horse, but by a secretariat. He would be armed, not by a lance, but with several flexible formulas....

"He would propose a conference with the dragon. He would then lend the dragon a lot of money. The maiden's release would be referred to Geneva or New York, the dragon reserving all rights meanwhile."

"What we need now is cool heads without cold hearts or cold feet."

— 1937

After the victory at El Alamein:

"I have never promised anything but blood, tears, toil, and sweat. Now, however, we have a new experience. We have a victory–a remarkable and definite victory. No, this is not the end. It is not even the beginning of the end. But it is, perhaps, the end of the beginning."

– London, 1942

On neutral nations:

"They bow humbly and in fear to German threats of violence, comforting themselves meanwhile with the thought that the Allies will win. Each one hopes that if he feeds the crocodile enough, the crocodile will eat him last. All of them hope that the storm will pass before their turn comes to be devoured."

– BBC broadcast, 1940

"We shall fight on the beaches. We shall fight on the landing grounds. We shall fight in the fields and in the streets. We shall fight in the hills; we shall never surrender. And [as an aside to a colleague, as the House rallied with cheers]... we will fight them with the butt end of broken bottles because that's bloody well all we've got."

– House of Commons, 1941

On Germany's growing defense superiority:

"We are a rich and easy prey. No country is so vulnerable, and no country would better repay pillage than our own... with our enormous Metropolis here, the greatest target in the world, a kind of tremendous, fat, valuable cow tied up to attract the beast of prey."

— *The Second World War, Volume I*

Referring to Hitler's past as a painter:

"Will you kindly explain to me the reasons which debar individuals in certain branches from rising by merit to commissioned rank? If a cook may rise, or a steward, why not an electrical artificer or an ordnance rating or a shipwright? If a telegraphist may rise, why not a painter? Apparently there is no difficulty about painters rising in Germany?"

— *The Second World War, Volume I*

"The argument is now put forward that we must never use the atomic bomb until, or unless, it has been used against us first. In other words, you must never fire until you have been shot dead. That seems to me a silly thing to say and a still more imprudent position to adopt."

— House of Commons, 1944

"Man is a gregarious animal, and apparently the mischievous microbes he exhales fight and neutralize each other. They go out and devour each other, and man walks off unharmed. If this is not scientifically correct, it ought to be."

– London, 1941

On the Japanese attack at Pearl Harbour:

"They have certainly embarked upon a very considerable undertaking."

– U.S. Congress, 1940

While the London Blitz raged, aide Brenden Bracken gave Churchill a newspaper article about a man of more than 75 years making improper advances to a girl in sub-zero weather.

"Over 75 and below zero! Makes you proud to be an Englishman."

– London, 1941

British night fighter pilots traditionally left the top button of their tunics open to distinguish themselves from bomber pilots. During an early morning visit, Churchill was reviewing a line of pilots who had hurriedly dressed for inspection. He spotted one pilot with his pants unbuttoned.

"Night fighters, I presume!"

– 1941

"It seems incongruous to record a joke in such somber scenes. But in war, the soldier's harsh laugh is often a measure of inward compressed emotions. The party were digging out a bomb, and their prize man had gone down the pit to perform the delicate act of disconnection. Suddenly, he shouted to be drawn up. Forward went his mates and pulled him out. They seized him by the shoulders and, dragging him along, all rushed off together for the 50 or 60 yards, which were supposed to give a chance. They flung themselves on the ground. But nothing happened. The prize man was seriously upset. He was blanched and breathless. They looked at him inquiringly. 'My God,' he said, 'there was a bloody great rat!'"

– *Second World War, Volume II*

In an exchange with Archbishop Cosmo Gordon Lang over the measures taken to protect Canterbury Cathedral during the London Blitz, Churchill couldn't resist a dig at the cleric, whom he disliked.

"What, my Lord Primate, are you doing to protect your sacred person against the bombs of our heathen foe?" Churchill asked.

"No more than other people, Prime Minister," Lang replied. "When the warning siren sounds I go to my shelter."

"But an ordinary shelter is by no means adequate in your case, Archbishop," Churchill said. "You owe it to the established church to take refuge in the cathedral crypt. There you would be quite safe. Unless of course there was a direct hit. Then I fear, my Lord Primate, you would have to regard that as a summons!"

"When I hear people talking in an airy way of throwing modern armies ashore here and there as if they were bales of goods, I marvel at the lack of knowledge of (the) conditions of modern war. This class of criticism, which I read in the paper, reminds me of the sailor who jumped into a dock to rescue a small boy from drowning. About a week later this sailor was accosted by a woman who asked, "Are you the man who picked my son out of the water the other night?"

The sailor replied modestly, "That is true, ma'am."

"Ah," said the woman, "you are the man I am looking for. Where is his cap?"

— *The Second World War, Volume V*

"'In wartime,' I said, 'truth is so precious that she should always be attended by a bodyguard of lies.' Stalin and his comrades greatly appreciated this remark when it was translated, and upon this note our formal conference ended gaily."

— Writing in *The Second World War, Volume V* about "Operation Overlord," the invasion of France, during the Teheran Conference with Joseph Stalin and Franklin D. Roosevelt.

"Let us learn our lessons: Never, never, never believe any war will be smooth and easy. Always remember, however sure you are that you can easily win, that there would not be war if the other man did not think he also had a chance."

– My Early Life

"Never, never, never believe any war will be smooth and easy, or that anyone who embarks on the strange voyage can measure the tides."

His pained response to his chief of staff, General Hastings (Pug) Ismay, on the many requests he could not fulfill for additional tanks, aircraft and materiel:

"It's the same old story, Pug, too many piglets and not enough teats."

"In war, the clouds never blow over; they gather unceasingly and fall in thunderbolts."

– The World Crisis

"War, disguise it as you may, is but a dirty, shoddy business, which only a fool would play at."

– *The Caged Lion: Winston Spencer Churchill 1932-1940* by William Raymond Manchester

Referring to the ceremonial declaration of war on Japan on December 8, 1941:

"When you have to kill a man, it costs nothing to be polite."

– 1950

"In war: resolution
In defeat: defiance
In victory: magnanimity
In peace: goodwill."

"It would be an unmeasured crime to prolong this war for one unnecessary day. It would be an unmeasured and immeasurable blunder to make peace before the vital objects are achieved."

"Let us to the task."

– Free Trade Hall, London, 1940

On World War II:

"There never was a war in all history easier to prevent by timely action."

"There is only one thing worse than fighting with allies, and that is fighting without them."

In appealing to the still neutral United States for military aid, Churchill referenced a poem that President Franklin D. Roosevelt had delivered to him:

"Here is the answer which I will give to President Roosevelt: We shall not fail or falter; we shall not weaken or tire. Give us the tools, and we will finish the job."

– BBC broadcast, 1941

When a haughty general asserted that "putting troops in the picture before a battle was the sort of familiarity which breeds contempt," Churchill responded:

"You know, general, without a certain amount of familiarity, it is extraordinarily difficult to breed anything at all."

After the attempt to establish a bridgehead at Anzio, Italy:

"We hoped to land a wildcat that would tear out the bowels of the Boche. Instead, we have stranded a vast whale with its tail flopping about in the water."

"We have not journeyed across the countries, across the oceans, across the mountains, across the prairies because we are made of sugar candy."

– Canadian House of Commons, 1941

"War is a game with a good deal of chance in it, and, from the little I have seen of it, I should say that nothing in war ever goes right, except by accident."

In response to the suggestion that Britian should prepare only for a defensive war:

"I cannot subscribe to the idea that it might be possible to dig ourselves in and make no preparations for anything other than passive defense. It is the theory of the turtle, which is disproved at every Lord Mayor's Banquet."

"He (Charles de Gaulle) reminds me of a female llama who has just been surprised in her bath."

PEOPLE

◆ ◆ ◆ ◆ ◆

On President Franklin D. Roosevelt's contention that the United Nations could be planned during the six days of talks at Yalta:

"I don't see any way of realizing our hopes for a World Organization in six days. Even the Almighty took seven."

Reportedly commenting on General Charles de Gaulle:

"The heaviest cross I have to bear is the Cross of Lorraine."

(Often attributed to Churchill, but, in all likelihood, the comment was made by Churchill's envoy to France, General Spears.)

Also on de Gaulle:

"He looks like a female llama who has just been surprised in her bath."

Orders to Field Marshal Sir Harold Alexander, commander in chief, Middle East:

1. Your prime and main duty will be to take or destroy at the earliest opportunity the German-Italian Army commanded by Field Marshal Rommel, together with all its supplies and establishments in Egypt and Libya.

2. You will discharge or cause to be discharged such other duties as pertain to your Command without prejudice to the task described in paragraph 1, which must be considered paramount in His Majesty's interests.

Six months later came the response from Alexander:

Alexander: "Sir, the Orders you gave me on August 10, 1942, have been fulfilled. His Majesty's enemies, together with their impedimenta, have been completely eliminated from Egypt, Cyrenaica, Libya, and Tripolitania. I now await your further instructions."

Churchill: "Well, obviously we shall have to think of something else!"

"Into that void strode a maniac of ferocious genius of the most virulent hatred that has ever corroded the human breast. . . Corporal Hitler."

"I hate nobody except Hitler–and that is professional."

"There is a winter, you know, in Russia. Hitler forgot about his Russian winter. He must have been very loosely educated. We all heard about it at school; but he forgot it. I have never made such a bad mistake as that."

— 1942

On allying with Russia, while still an implacable foe of Communism:

"If Hitler invaded hell, I would make at least a favourable reference to the devil in the House of Commons."

"In the summer of 1932 for the purposes of my life of Marlborough I visited his old battlefields in the Low Countries and Germany. At the Regina Hotel (in Munich) a gentleman introduced himself. He was Herr Hanfstaengl and spoke a great deal about "the Fuehrer," with whom he appeared to be intimate. He said I ought to meet him. However, in the course of conversation with Hanfstaengl I happened to say, 'Why is your chief so violent about the Jews? I can quite understand being angry with Jews who have done wrong or are against the country, and I understand resisting them if they try to monopolize power in any walk of life; but what is the sense of being against a man simply because of his birth? How can any man help how he is born?'

"He must have repeated this to Hitler, because about noon the next day he came around with a rather serious air and said that the appointment he had made for me to meet Hitler could not take place. Thus, Hitler lost his only chance of meeting me. Later on when he was all-powerful, I was to receive several invitations from him. But by that time a lot had happened, and I excused myself."

"I will have you know that as a child my nurse maid could never prevent me from taking a walk in the park if I wanted to do so. And as a man, Adolf Hitler certainly won't."

– London, 1941

"Hitler has told us that it was a crime in such circumstances on our part to go to the aid of the Greeks. I do not wish to enter into argument with experts."

– House of Commons, 1941

Entering a men's room in the House of Commons, he encountered Labour Party leader Clement Attlee. Churchill walked to the far end of a long row of urinals.

Attlee: "Winston, I know we're political opponents, but we don't have to carry our differences into the gentlemen's lavatory."

Churchill: "Clement, the trouble with you Socialists is that whenever you see anything in robust and sturdy condition you want the government to regulate it."

⁓

Also on Attlee:

"A sheep in sheep's clothing."

⁓

Again on Attlee:

"He is a modest man who has a good deal to be modest about."

On former Prime Minister Stanley Baldwin:

"He occasionally stumbled over the truth, but hastily picked himself up and hurried on as if nothing had happened."

– 1936

Baldwin once remarked that Churchill "cannot really tell lies. That is what makes him so bad a conspirator."

On Prime Minister Arthur Balfour:

"He passed from one cabinet to the other, from the Prime Minister [Herbert H. Asquith] who was his champion to the Prime Minister [Lloyd George] who had been his most severe critic, like a powerful graceful cat walking delicately and unsoiled across a rather muddy street."

– *Great Contemporaries*

"There but for the grace of God goes God."

– *Winston Churchill* by Piers Brendon

On R.A. Butler, Conservative chancellor of the Exchequer:

"I am amused by the Chancellor of the Exchequer. He is always patting himself on the back, a kind of exercise that contributes to his excellent physical condition."

❦

Commenting on protectionist politician Joseph Chamberlain's rejection of free trade:

"Mr. Chamberlain loves the working man; he loves to see him work."

ↄ

On Prime Minister Neville Chamberlain:

"In the depths of that dusty soul, there is nothing but abject surrender."

To Chamberlain after the Munich Settlement of 1938:

"You were given the choice between war and dishonour. You chose dishonour, and you will have war."

When a colleague likened Neville Chamberlain's attempt to force Attlee to accept the Munich appeasement to a snake dominating a rabbit, Churchill surmised:

"It's more like a rabbit dominating a lettuce!"

Also on the Munich appeasement:

"We have sustained a defeat without a war."

– House of Commons

"The country thought Mr. Chamberlain was a prophet with a message. They found him a politician groping for a platform."

During a photo session for his 75th birthday, a photographer said, "I hope to have the opportunity to take your photograph on your 100th birthday." Churchill replied:

"I don't see why not young man. You look healthy enough."

The quip was reportedly repeated five years later:

While having his photo taken on his 80th birthday, a photographer said, "Sir Winston, it is wonderful to take your photograph on your 80th birthday and I do look forward to taking it again on your hundredth birthday."

"Young man," Churchill responded, "you appear to me to be in good health and sound in wind and limb. So I see no reason why you should not."

Churchill to American author Winston Churchill:

"Mr. Winston Churchill presents his compliments to Mr. Winston Churchill, and begs to draw his attention to a matter which concerns them both. He has learnt from the Press notices that Mr. Winston Churchill proposes to bring out another novel, entitled "Richard Carvel," which is certain to have a considerable sale both in England and America. Mr. Winston Churchill is also the author of a novel now being published in serial form in "Macmillan's Magazine," and for which he anticipates some sale both in England and America. He also proposes to publish on the 1st of October another military chronicle on the Soudan War. He has no doubt that Mr. Winston Churchill will recognize from his letter–if indeed by no other means–that there is grave danger of his works being mistaken for those of Mr. Winston Churchill. He feels sure that Mr. Winston Churchill desires this as little as he does himself. In future to avoid mistakes as far as possible, Mr. Winston Churchill has decided to sign all published articles, stories, or other works, "Winston Spencer Churchill", and not "Winston Churchill" as formerly. He trusts that this arrangement will commend itself to Mr. Winston Churchill, and he ventures to suggest, with a view to preventing further confusion which may arise out of this extraordinary coincidence, that both Mr. Winston Churchill and Mr. Winston Churchill should insert a short note in their respective publications explaining to the public which are the works of Mr. Winston Churchill and which are those of Mr. Winston Churchill. The text of this note might form a subject for future discussion if Mr. Winston Churchill agrees with Mr. Winston Churchill upon the style and success of his works, which are always brought to his notice whether in magazine or book form, and he trusts that Mr. Winston Churchill has derived equal pleasure from any work of his that may have attracted his attention."

– A Roving Commission

During a disagreement with U.S. diplomat John Foster Dulles:

"He is the only case of a bull I know who carries his china closet with him."

Again on Dulles:

"Dull, duller, Dulles."

– *Winston Churchill* by Piers Brendon

❋

A cabled exchange between Churchill and Anthony Eden, Lord Avon, charged with bringing Turkey into the war:

Eden: "Progress slow. What more can I tell Turkey?"

Churchill: "Tell them Christmas is coming!"

Remarking to his daughter Sarah on being embraced by Turkish President Inönü during a farewell ceremony:

"Do you know what happened to me today? The Turkish president kissed me. The truth is I'm irresistible. But don't tell Anthony (Eden); he's jealous."

On U.S. General Dwight D. Eisenhower

"He is a prairie prince. A man who set the unity of the Allied Armed Forces above all nationalistic thought."

On friend and Prime Minister Lloyd George:

"The Happy Warrior of Squandermania."

On farming at Chartwell:

"I'm going to make it pay, whatever it costs."

— 1924

On the Earl of Halifax, British foreign secretary from 1939-1940:

"Halifax's virtues have done more harm than the vices of hundreds of other people."

On Rudolf Hess:

"He is the maggot in the Nazi apple."

— *Portrait of Churchill* by Guy Eden

On Soviet leader Vladimir Ilyich Lenin:

"Lenin was sent to Russia by the Germans in the same way that you might send a phial containing a culture of typhoid or cholera to be poured into the water supply of a great city, and it worked with amazing accuracy."

– House of Commons, 1919

Also on Lenin:

"He alone could have led Russia into the enchanted quagmire. He alone could have found the way back to the causeway. He saw; he turned; he perished. The Russian people were left floundering in the bog. Their worst misfortune was his birth, their next worst–his death."

Lenin once more:

"Implacable vengeance rising from a frozen pity; his sympathies cold and wide as the Arctic Ocean; his hatreds right as the hangman's noose. His purpose, to save the world; his method, to blow it up."

On Lawrence of Arabia:

"He was not in complete harmony with the normal."

On Soviet Foreign Secretary Vyacheslav Molotov:

"I have never seen a human being who more perfectly represented the modern conception of a robot."

German General Wilhelm von Thomas was captured in North Africa. His captor, General Montgomery, invited him to dinner one evening, evoking outrage in Britain. Churchill remarked:

"I sympathize with General von Thomas: defeated, humiliated, in captivity, and dinner with General Montgomery."

On Italian leader Benito Mussolini:

"The hyena in its nature broke all bounds of decency and common sense."

In a margin note on a report from Admiral Sir Dudley Pound:
"Pennywise."

In a quip about Greek General Plastiras:
"Plasterarse, eh? Well, I hope at least he hasn't got feet of clay."

– During the Greek civil war, 1944

Churchill was not pleased when daughter Sarah married entertainer Vic Oliver.

Oliver once asked him who was the greatest statesman Churchill had known. Churchill replied, "Benito Mussolini."

"Why Mussolini?" Oliver asked.

"He had the courage to have his son-in-law shot," Churchill answered.

"I turn aside from the stony path we have to tread, to indulge a moment of lighter relief. I daresay you have read in the newspapers that by a special proclamation, the Italian dictator had congratulated the Italian army in Albania on the glorious laurels they have gained by their victory over the Greeks. Here surely is the world's record in the domain of the ridiculous and the contemptible. This whipped jackal, Mussolini, who to save his own skin has made all Italy a vassal state of Hitler's empire, comes frisking up at the side of the German tiger with yelpings not only of appetite— that can be understood—but even of triumph."

– BBC, 1941

On President Franklin D. Roosevelt:

"Meeting him was like opening your first bottle of champagne. That great man whom destiny has marked for the climax of human fortune. He was the greatest friend Britain ever had. He died on the wings of victory, but he saw them and heard them beating."

༄

Again on President Roosevelt:

"I shall not hesitate to affirm, and indeed to repeat, that he was the greatest American friend that Britain ever found and the foremost champion of freedom and justice who has ever stretched strong hands across the oceans to rescue Europe and Asia from tyranny and destruction."

– London, 1948

༄

Upon arriving at Normandy shortly after the D-Day invasion, Churchill sent President Roosevelt a postcard, saying "Wish you were here."

– 1944

While visiting the White House, President Roosevelt rolled himself in his wheelchair into Churchill's room and surprised the prime minister emerging naked from the bath. He quickly tried to exit the room, but Churchill stopped him, saying:

"The prime minister has nothing to hide from the president of the United States."

At a White House dinner, South African official Jan Smuts told of receiving a letter from Churchill 47 years earlier asking that Smuts free him from imprisonment as a war correspondent. Before General Smuts could respond, Churchill escaped. They later became friends.

Churchill: "Because you were so slow I made nine thousand pounds."

Smuts: "Nine thousand pounds!"

Churchill: "That's what I was paid for the story of my escape."

With anti-German sentiment running high, Churchill had to decline the volunteered service of Humbert Wolfe, a British poet of Austrian descent:

"Ah Humbert! Hun-wept. Hun-honoured and Hun-sung."

– 1914

On Russian Communist leader Leon Trotsky:

"He sits disconsolate–a skin of malice stranded for a time on the shores of the Black Sea and now washed up in the Gulf of Mexico. He possessed in his nature all the qualities requisite for the art of civic destruction–the organizing command of a Carnot, the cold detached intelligence of a Machiavelli, the mob oratory of a Cleon, the ferocity of a Jack the Ripper, the toughness of Titus Oates."

— *Great Contemporaries*

౿

Again on Trotsky:

"In the deepest depth he sought with desperate energy for a deeper. But–poor wretch–he had reached rock bottom. Nothing lower than the Communist criminal class could be found."

— *Great Contemporaries*

౿

"I must confess that I never liked Trotsky."

— House of Commons, 1944

On President Harry S. Truman:

"He seems a man of exceptional character and ability, [possessing] simple and direct methods of speech and a great deal of self-confidence and resolution."

George Bernard Shaw sent two tickets for his upcoming play to Churchill with the message, "Bring a friend if you have one."

Churchill responded that he was unable to attend the opening performance, but he would like two tickets for the second night, "if there is one."

On rumors in 1951 that he had died:

"I am informed from many quarters that a rumour has been put about that I died this morning. This is quite untrue."

– *My Years with Churchill* by Norman McGowan

"Trying to maintain good relations with the Communists
is like wooing a crocodile. You do not know whether to
tickle it under the chin or beat it over the head."

Socialism & Communism
◆ ◆ ◆ ◆ ◆

"Socialism is the philosophy of failure, the creed of ignorance, and the gospel of envy."

"The inherent vice of Capitalism is the unequal sharing of blessings; the inherent virtue of Socialism is the equal sharing of miseries."

— House of Commons, 1945

Commenting on the proposition of calling food stations "Communal Feeding Centres:"

"I hope the term Communal Feeding Centres is not going to be adopted. It is an odious expression, suggestive of Communism and the workhouse. I suggest you call them 'British Restaurants.' Everybody associates the word 'restaurant' with a good meal, and they may as well have the name if they cannot get anything else."

— *The Second World War, Volume III*

"I hope you have all mastered the official Socialist jargon, which our masters, as they call themselves, wish us to learn. You must not use the word 'poor;' they are described as the 'lower income group.' When it comes to a question of freezing a workman's wages, the chancellor of the exchequer speaks of 'arresting increases in personal income.' The idea is that formerly income tax payers used to be the well-to-do, and that therefore it will be popular and safe to hit at them. Sir Stafford Cripps does not like to mention the word 'wages,' but that is what he means. There is a lovely one about houses and homes. They are in future to be called 'accommodation units.' I don't know how we are to sing our old song *Home Sweet Home*. 'Accommodations Unit, Sweet Accommodation Unit.' I hope to live to see the British Democracy spit all this rubbish from their lips."

– Election speech, 1950

On the H-bomb:

"Some of the Socialists say that it should be made and tested, but not used until we have first been attacked by this kind of weapon. That would be like a man saying: 'I carry a pistol in self-defence, but you can trust me not to use it until I am shot dead.'"

– Election speech, 1955

"I do not wonder that British youth is in revolt against the morbid doctrine that nothing matters but the equal sharing of miseries; that what used to be called the submerged tenth can only be rescued by bringing the other nine-tenths down to their level, against the folly that it is better that everyone should have half rations rather than that any by their exertions, or ability, should earn a second helping."

A Socialist, praising the successes of the system, cited the increase in population under the three years of Labourite administration. Churchill responded:

"Wouldn't the honourable gentleman concede that the last statistic about population is due to private enterprise?"

"'All men are created equal,' says the American Declaration of Independence. 'All men shall be kept equal,' say the British Socialist Party."

– Election speech, 1957

"Let there be sunshine on both sides of the Iron Curtain; and if ever the sunshine should be equal on both sides, the Curtain will be no more."

"Trying to maintain good relations with the Communists is like wooing a crocodile. You do not know whether to tickle it under the chin or beat it over the head. When it opens its mouth you cannot tell whether it is trying to smile or preparing to eat you up."

"There is not one single social or economic principle or concept in the philosophy of the Russian Bolshevik which has not been realized, carried into action, and enshrined in immutable laws a million years ago by the white ant."

On Bolshevism:

"A ghoul descending from a pile of skulls."

"They [the Germans] turned upon Russia the most grisly of all weapons. They transported Lenin in a sealed truck like a plague bacillus from Switzerland into Russia."

"I cannot forecast to you the action of Russia. It is a riddle wrapped in a mystery inside an enigma, but perhaps there is a key. That key is Russian national interest."

– 1939

During a speech, Churchill dismissed a Socialist MP's interruption in rebuttal:

"I do not challenge the honourable gentleman when the truth leaks out of him by accident from time to time."

"Victory will never be found by taking the
line of least resistance."

LEADERSHIP

◆ ◆ ◆ ◆ ◆

"I have never accepted what many people have kindly said, namely that I inspired the nation. Their will was resolute and remorseless, and as it proved, unconquerable. It was the nation and the race dwelling all round the globe that had the lion's heart. I had the luck to be called upon to give the roar!"

– Palace of Westminster, 1954

"Nothing is more dangerous in wartime than to live in the temperamental atmosphere of a Gallup Poll, always feeling one's pulse and taking one's temperature. I see that a speaker at the weekend said that this was a time when leaders should keep their ears to the ground. All I can say is that the British nation will find it very hard to look up to leaders who are detected in that somewhat ungainly posture."

– House of Commons

"It is no use saying 'We are doing our best.' You have to succeed in doing what is necessary."

On brinksmanship:

"It is no use leading other nations up the garden and then running away when the dog growls."

"Courage is rightly esteemed the first of human qualities because it is the quality which guarantees all others."

"There is a precipice on either side of you–a precipice of caution and a precipice of over-daring."

"It is no good going to the country solely on the platform of your opponents' mistakes."

On Prime Minister Arthur Balfour's attempt to separate himself from the various opposed party factions:

"The dignity of a prime minister, like a lady's virtue, is not susceptible of partial diminution."

– House of Commons, 1905

"I cannot subscribe to the idea that it might be possible to dig ourselves in and make no preparations for anything else than passive defence. It is the theory of the turtle."

"Any clever person can make plans for winning a war if he has no responsibility for carrying them out."

On the RMS Queen Mary, referring to his "Iron Curtain" speech:

"You remember Fulton. I got into great trouble being a bit in front of the weather that time. But it's all come out since– I won't say right, but it's all come out."

– 1953

Asked by the queen if he was considering retirement:

"Not until I'm a great deal worse, and the Empire a great deal better."

– 1953

"Thoughtless, dilettante or purblind worldlings sometimes ask us, 'What is it that Britain and France are fighting for?' To this I answer, 'If we left off fighting, you would soon find out.'"

Commenting on growing military might and the reluctance of Prime Minister Stanley Baldwin and other British officials to confront Hitler:

"The First Lord of the Admiralty [Sir Samuel Hoare] said...everything is fluid. The government simply cannot make up their minds, or they cannot get the prime minister to make up his mind. So they go on in strange paradox, decided only to be undecided, resolved to be irresolute, adamant for drift, solid for fluidity, all powerful to be impotent. So we go on preparing more months and years— precious perhaps vital to the greatness of Britain for the locusts to eat."

– House of Commons, 1936

"If we go on waiting upon events, how much shall we throw away our resources now available for our security?"

A little boy visiting Chartwell was told by his nanny that he was going to meet the greatest man in the world. While the nanny took tea, her young charge stole into Churchill's room to find him reading.

"Are you the greatest man in the whole wide world?" the lad asked.

"Of course I'm the greatest man in the whole wide world," Churchill said. "Now buzz off."

(This anecdote appears often with a different little boy.)

"Democracy is the occasional necessity of deferring to the opinions of other people."

"It is an error to believe that the world began when any particular party or statesman got into office. It has all been going on quite a long time."

During a discussion about mistakes made at the Yalta and Potsdam conferences.

"Let us stop our melancholy recriminations and apply ourselves to the business at hand. Let us leave hindsight to history—that history which I am now, myself, in the process of writing!"

– House of Commons, 1947

"Statesmen are not called upon to settle the easy questions; these often settle themselves. It is when the balance quivers and the proportions are veiled in mist that the opportunities for world-saving decisions present themselves."

"Criticism in the body politic is like pain in the human body. It is not pleasant but where would the body be without it?"

"The world today is ruled by harassed politicians absorbed in getting into office or turning out the other man so that not much room is left for debating great issues on their merits."

"We mean to hold our own. I have not become the King's First Minister in order to preside over the liquidation of the British Empire. For that task, if ever it were prescribed, someone else would have to be consulted."

– London, 1942

Following his defeat for re-election as prime minister in 1945, Churchill was informed that King George wanted to bestow on him the Order of the Garter–the highest knightly honor.

"Why should I accept the Order of the Garter from my sovereign when I have already received from the people the Order of the Boot?"

While being called upon at Yalta to make a toast to Soviet leader Joseph Stalin, Churchill noted to an aide "But they do not want peace." Under pressure, he rose to give the toast nonetheless:

"To Premier Stalin, whose conduct of foreign policy manifests a desire for peace."

Outside the hearing of the translator, he said, "A piece of Poland, a piece of Czechoslovakia, a piece of Romania...."

"In critical and baffling situations, it is always best to return to first principle and simple action."

"I did not suffer from any desire to be relieved of my responsibilities. All I wanted was a compliance with my wishes after reasonable discussion."

– *The Second World War, Volume V*

"I found that I could add nearly two hours to my working day by going to bed for an hour after luncheon."

– *My Early Life*

"All the greatest things are simple, and many can be expressed in a single word: freedom, justice, honour, duty, mercy, hope."

– London, 1947

"It is one thing to feel confident, and it is another to impart that confidence to people who do not like your plan, and who feel the same confidence in their knowledge as you do in yours."

– House of Commons, 1925

"It is no use doing what you like; you have to like what you do…. Human beings may be divided into three classes: those who are toiled to death, those who are worried to death, and those who are bored to death."

– *Thoughts and Adventures*

Upon being named prime minister in May 1940:

"[I was] conscious of a profound source of relief. I felt as if I was walking with destiny, and that all my past life had been but a preparation for this hour and this trial."

"On the night of the tenth of May [1940], at the outset of this mighty battle, I acquired the chief power in the state, which henceforth I wielded in ever-growing measure for five years and three months of world war, at the end of which time, all our enemies having surrendered unconditionally or being about to do so, I was immediately dismissed by the British electorate from all further conduct of their affairs."

– *The Second World War, Volume I*

"The best method of acquiring flexibility is to have three or four plans for all the probable contingencies all worded out with the utmost detail. Then it is much easier to switch from one to the other as to when and where the cat jumps."

"Success cannot be guaranteed. There are no safe battles."

"Victory will never be found by taking the line of least resistance."

*"All dogs look up to you. All cats look down on you.
Only a pig looks at you as an equal."*

ANIMALS

• • • • •

Churchill was fond of all animals. Commenting to his wife,
Clementine, before lunch one Sunday of a goose raised at Chartwell:

"You carve him, Clemmie; he was my friend."

– 1932

On another occasion when served a Christmas goose from his own
stock, he put down his knife and fork:

"I could not possibly eat a bird that I have known socially."

"Odd things animals. All dogs look up to you. All cats look
down on you. Only a pig looks at you as an equal."

"The British lion, so fierce and valiant in bygone days, so
dauntless and unconquerable through all the agony of
Armageddon, can now be chased by rabbits from the fields
and forests of his former glory."

– *Liverpool, 1931*

Describing his naval strategy in World War I that led to sinking three German cruisers and disabling five others while also moving the British Expeditionary Force to France:

"The nose of the bulldog has been slanted backward so that he can breathe without letting go!"

– 1914

Upon learning that his dining partner Violet Asquith was only 19 years old:

"And I am already 33. Curse ruthless time! Curse our mortality! How cruelly short is the allotted span for all we must cram into it! We are all worms.
But I do believe that I am a glow worm."

– *Winston Churchill, An Intimate Portrait* by Violet Bonham Carter

"I have always considered that the substitution of the internal combustion machine for the horse marked a very gloomy milestone in the progress of mankind."

– House of Commons, 1952

During his illness in North Africa in 1943, doctors repeatedly took blood samples from his ears and were unable to draw more. They were puzzled as to where else to take their samples.

"Never let it be said that I have a human vampire and refuse to feed him. It is true that I have two ears, but I also have 10 fingers and 10 toes–and an infinite expanse of bottom!"

While traveling with President Harry S. Truman by train to make his famous Iron Curtain speech at Westminster College in Fulton, Missouri, Churchill noted the presidential seal mounted in Truman's club car. The seal showed the eagle with a quiver of arrows in one talon and the olive branch in the other. Its head was turned toward the arrows. Truman explained that he had ordered that the seal be altered to have the eagle face the olive branch of peace.

Churchill asked, "Why not put the eagle's neck on a swivel so that it could turn to the right or left as the occasion presented itself?"

– 1946

On being invited by the Chamberlain Cabinet to meet German Ambassador Joachim von Ribbentrop:

"I suppose they asked me to show him that, if they couldn't bark themselves, they kept a dog which could bark and might bite."

– 1938

A disarmament fable:

"Once upon a time, all the animals in the zoo decided that they would disarm, and they arranged to have a conference to arrange the matter. So, the rhinoceros said when he opened the proceedings that the use of teeth was barbarous and horrible and ought to be strictly prohibited by general consent. Horns, which were mainly defensive weapons, would of course, have to be allowed. The buffalo, the stag, the porcupine, and even the little hedgehog all said they would vote with the rhino, but the lion and the tiger took a different view. They defended teeth and even claws, which they described as honourable weapons of immemorial antiquity. The panther, the leopard, the puma, and the whole tribe of small cats all supported the lion and the tiger. Then the bear spoke. He proposed that both teeth and horns should be banned and never used again for fighting by any animal. It would be quite enough if animals were allowed to give each other a good hug when they quarreled.

No one could object to that. It was so fraternal, and that would be a great step towards peace. However, all the other animals were very offended with the bear, and the turkey fell into a perfect panic.

"The discussion got so hot and angry, and all those animals began thinking so much about horns and teeth and hugging when they argued about the peaceful intentions that had brought them together that they began to look at one another in a very nasty way. Luckily the keepers were able to calm them down and persuade them to go back quietly to their cages, and they began to feel quite friendly with one another again."

Describing how he spent his earnings from his first American lecture tour:

"I sent my 10,000 pounds to my father's old friend, Sir Ernest Cassel, with the instruction, 'Feed my sheep.' He fed the sheep with great prudence. They did not multiply fast, but they fattened steadily, and none of them ever died. Indeed from year to year they had a few lambs; but these were not numerous enough for me to live upon. I had every year to eat a sheep or two as well; so gradually my flock grew smaller, until in a few years, it was almost entirely devoured. Nevertheless, while it lasted, I had no care."

— *A Roving Commission*

❧

"The manner of killing a rhinoceros in the open is crudely simple. It is thought well usually to select the neighbourhood of a good tree, where one can be found, as the centre of the encounter. If no tree is available, you walk up as near as possible to him from any side except the windward, and then shoot him in the head or the heart. If you hit a vital spot, as sometimes happens, he falls. If you hit him anywhere else, he charges blindly and furiously in your direction, and you shoot him again, or not, as the case may be."

— *My African Journey*

Regarding his horse Colonist II, which raced in Churchill's colors, pink and chocolate:

"I told him this is a very big race, and if you win it, you will never have to run again. You will spend the rest of your life in agreeable female company.

"Colonist II did not keep his mind on the race."

On a trip in 1907 to Aden, he was given a camel prone to kicking and bad humor. After a while, a Somali boy reported to Churchill's undersecretary for the colonies, Edward (Eddie) Marsh:

"Sahib, camel kick Churchill; Churchill, Sahib, kick camel. Him very good camel now, Sahib."

After 107 miles on the march, Churchill said to Marsh, "So fari; so goodie!"

— *A Biography of Edward March* by Christopher Hassall

"Where does a family start? It starts with a young man falling in love with a girl–no superior alternative has yet been found."

WOMEN

◆ ◆ ◆ ◆ ◆

"If I could not be who I am, I would most like to be... Mrs.
Churchill's second husband."

*His mother's friend expressed dislike of his politics as well as the
mustache he grew after his capture in the Boer War.*

"Madam, I see no earthly reason why you should come in
contact with either."

*Commenting on women chaining themselves to railings in support of
gaining the right to vote:*

"I might as well chain myself to St. Thomas's [Hospital] and
say I would not move until I had a baby."

(Later as Home Secretary, Churchill signed an order
appointing women for several executive positions, saying
"Let there be women!")

While overseeing the pouring of coffee at a dinner party at Lady Nancy Astor's mansion, she caught Churchill's eye and declared, "Winston, if I were your wife, I'd put poison in your coffee."

"Nancy," Churchill replied, "if I were your husband, I'd drink it."

– The Wit & Wisdom of Winston Churchill

ر

When Lady Astor, an American, became the first female member of Parliament, Churchill commented:

"Nancy, when you entered the House, I felt you had come upon me in my bath, and I had nothing to protect me but my sponge."

ڕ

"We have never been likely to get into trouble by having an extra thousand or two of up-to-date aeroplanes at our disposal.... As the man whose mother-in-law had died in Brazil replied when asked how the remains should be disposed of, 'Embalm, cremate, and bury. Take no risks!'"

– 1938

"It's an extraordinary business, this way of bringing babies into the world. I don't know how God thought of it."

During a speaking tour of the United States in 1900, Churchill encountered a very amply endowed woman from Richmond, Virginia. She proudly noted her family's resistance to Reconstruction: "Mr. Churchill, you see before you a rebel who has not been reconstructed."

"Madam," he responded, "reconstruction in your case would be blasphemous."

"My mother always seemed to me a fairy princess—a radiant being possessed of limitless riches and power. She shone for me like the Evening Star. I loved her dearly but at a distance."

"Where does a family start? It starts with a young man falling in love with a girl—no superior alternative has yet been found."

– House of Commons, 1936

To his wife, Clementine:

"Twelve times I have seen your birthday come and each time your gracious beauty and loving charm have made a deeper impression on my heart. God bless you, darling, in the year that opens and give you happiness which fills your life.

"The most precious thing I have in life is your love for me.

"I love you more each month that passes and feel the need of you and your beauty…. I am so devoured of egoism that I would like to have another soul in another world and meet you in another setting and pay you all the love and honor of the great romances."

Churchill was the guest of honor at a dinner reception in Richmond, Virginia. When the buxom hostess offered him chicken, he asked for a breast. As she served his plate, the hostess explained, "We Southern ladies use the term "white meat."

The following day, Churchill sent her a corsage and a note: "I would be most obliged if you would pin this on your 'white meat.'"

"My wife and I tried two or three times in the last few years to have breakfast together but it was so disagreeable we had to stop.

"Breakfast should be in bed alone."

"In September 1908, I married and lived happily ever after."

– *My Early Life*

"My most brilliant achievement was to persuade my wife to marry me."

*"I have had to eat my words on occasion
and on the whole, I have found them quite tasty."*

Oratory & Words

◆ ◆ ◆ ◆ ◆

When asked if he wasn't delighted to find that his speeches produced overflow crowds:

"It is quite flattering. But whenever I feel this way I always remember that if instead of making a political speech I was being hanged, the crowd would be twice as big."

– *My Years with Churchill* by Norman McGowan

Interrupting a member of Parliament's meandering monologue against Churchill's wartime policies:

"I must warn him that he runs a very grave risk of falling into senility before he is overtaken by age."

"I am going to speak in French, a formidable undertaking and one which will put great demands on your friendship with Great Britain."

– Speech at the Liberation of Paris, 1944

Commenting on the first public address by the son of a disliked Conservative government minister:

"Isn't it enough to have this parent volcano continually erupting in our midst? And now we are to have these subsidiary craters spouting forth the same unhealthy fumes."

– *Churchill, by His Contemporaries* by Charles Eade

"The honourable member is never lucky in the coincidence of his facts with the truth."

– House of Commons, 1954

During a long speech by a Labor MP, Churchill rested his head on his chest and closed his eyes. The action sparked an accusation from the speaker that Churchill was asleep.

"I wish to God I were!" Churchill replied.

On another such occasion:

"Must you fall asleep when I am speaking?" a Labour MP railed.

"No," Churchill retorted. "It is purely voluntary."

Remarking on a long-winded speech by an academic Socialist:

"Verbosity may be the long suit of the honourable gentleman, but it's not long enough to cover his ass-ininity."

Responding to a question from his personal assistant, Commander C.R. Thompson, on how he was able to give so many speeches with only topic headings as guides:

"It isn't nearly as difficult as you think. I just start my mouth off talking and leave it."

– 1941

Churchill's Nobel Prize acceptance speech as read December 10, 1953, by Lady Churchill in Stockholm:

"The roll on which my name has been inscribed represents much that is outstanding in the world's literature of the 20th century. I am proud, but also I must admit, awestruck at your decision to include me. I do hope you are right. I feel we are both running a considerable risk and that I do not deserve it. But I shall have no misgivings if you have none."

"This Treasury paper, by its very length, defends itself against the risk of being read."

    — Churchill: Taken from The Diaries of Lord Moran: The Struggle for Survival 1940-1965
by Charles McMoran Wilson Moran

🕉

In his first political speech in 1897 to the Conservative Primrose League at Claverton Manor, he was allotted 15 minutes to speak; he planned to use 25.

"One must not yield too easily to the weaknesses of audiences. There they were; what could they do? They had asked for it, and they must have it."

ᒼ

In that first speech:

"England would gain far more from the rising tide of Tory Democracy than from the dried-up drainpipe of radicalism."

    — A Roving Commission

ᒼᔭ

"It is often said that facts are stubborn things."

    — "The Deterrent–Nuclear Warfare," 1955

*Answering criticism of him as the First Lord of the Admiralty from
Lord Charles Beresford:*

"He can best be described as one of those orators who,
before they get up, do not know what they are going to say;
when they are speaking, do not know what they are saying;
and when they have sat down, do not know what they
have said."

– House of Commons, 1911

"Here I say very little of the Prime Minister's
[Ramsay MacDonald] oratorical style. We are familiar with it
here. We know that he has, more than any other man, the
gift of compressing the largest number of words into the
smallest amount of thought."

– 1933

Upon the first speech by the witty A.P. Herbert, an Independent MP:

"Call that a maiden speech? It was a brazen hussy of a
speech. Never did such a painted lady of a speech parade
itself before a modest Parliament!"

– 1935

"My idea of a good dinner is, first to have good food, then discuss good food, and after this good food has been elaborately discussed, to discuss a good topic– with myself as chief conversationalist."

"Apt analogies are among the most formidable weapons of the rhetorician."

On orators:

"Before he can inspire them with any emotion, he must be swayed by it himself. When he would rouse their indignation, his heart is filled with anger. Before he can move their tears, his own must flow. To convince them, he must himself believe. His opinions may change as their impressions fade but every orator means what he says at that moment he says it. He may be often inconsistent. He is never consciously insincere."

"It was my ambition all my life to be master of the spoken word."

After giving a speech at a banquet attended by Churchill, a young MP asked how he performed:

> "First, you read the speech. Secondly, you read it badly. Finally, it wasn't a speech worth reading!"

༄

Churchill often prepared his speeches in bed, noting those that took considerable effort:

> "This speech is hanging over me like a vulture."

And

> "I'm going to make a long speech because I've not had the time to prepare a short one."

"Let us not shrink from using the short expressive phrase even if it is conversational."

"When I warned them [the French] that Britain would fight on alone whatever they did, their generals told their prime minister and his divided cabinet: 'In three weeks England will have her neck wrung like a chicken.' Some chicken! Some neck!"

– Ottawa, 1941.

(The comment also sparked laughter and applause because, unknown to Churchill at the time, the word "neck" was slang to Canadians for "nerve.")

Criticizing members of the House of Lords:

"It is a poor sport–almost like teasing goldfish. There is no sport whatever in catching them. It would be barbarous to leave them gasping on the bank of public ridicule, upon which they have landed themselves. Let us put them back gently, tenderly into their fountains–and if a few bright scales have been rubbed off in what the prime minister calls the variegated handling they have received, they will soon get over it."

– Lancaster, 1909

Rebuking an MP who repeatedly rose to his feet to interrupt one of Churchill's speeches:

"The honourable gentleman should really not generate more indignation than he can conveniently contain."

Responding to a reporter who asked what were the most difficult tasks in his life:

"To climb a ladder leaning towards you, to kiss a girl leaning away from you, and third, to give an after-dinner speech."

At a Conservative Party conference, he noted data produced by Food Minister Gwilym Lloyd George:

"But he found time to work out this fact, which I asked for because I knew it would be plain and simple and could be well understood even by collective ideologists, those professional intellectuals who revel in demand and polysyllables. Personally I like short words and vulgar fractions. Here is the plain vulgar fact."

When asked by an American general to critique a speech he had written: "Too many passives and too many zeds."

After being asked to clarify, Churchill elaborated: "Too many Latinate polysyllabics like 'systematize', 'prioritize' and 'finalize'. And then the passives. What if I had said, instead of 'We shall fight on the beaches,' 'Hostilities will be engaged with our adversary on the coastal perimeter'?"

"Eating my words has never given me indigestion."

First speech as prime minister:
"I have nothing to offer you but blood, toil, tears, and sweat."

– 1940

On this 75th birthday:
"I am ready to meet my Maker. Whether my Maker is prepared for the great ordeal of meeting me is another matter."

– 1951

"I was once asked to devise an inscription for a monument in France. I wrote, 'In war, Resolution. In defeat, Defiance. In victory, Magnanimity. In peace, Goodwill.' The inscription was not accepted. It is all the fault of the human brain being made in two lobes, only one of which does any thinking, so that we are all right-handed or left-handed; whereas, if we were properly constructed, we should use our right and left hands with equal force and skill according to circumstances. As it is, those who can win a war well can rarely make a good peace, and those who could make a good peace would never have won the war. It would perhaps be pressing the argument too far to suggest that I could do both."

– My Early Life

Describing the Lend Lease program:

"The most unsordid act."

"I am biased in favour of boys learning English. I would let the clever ones learn Latin as an honour, and Greek as a treat. But the only thing I would whip them for is for not knowing English. I would whip them hard for that."

– My Early Life

"The Chinese labour contract cannot, in the opinion of his majesty's government, be classified as slavery in the extreme acceptance of the word without some risk of terminological inexactitude."

— House of Commons, 1906

Following in the tradition of many speakers in the House of Commons who had learned Latin in public school, Churchill opted on one occasion to turn a Latin phrase. "I will now proceed to translate for the benefit of those…" he said, pausing.

Labour members, expecting to be lambasted with the phrase "lacking the advantage of a public school education," were surprised as Churchill continued, "for the benefit of any old Etonians who may be present."

Upon learning that venereal disease was spreading rapidly in Africa in 1907:

"Ah, Pox Britannica!"

"I have been wondering, Mr. Speaker, in all the circumstances, you would have permitted me to call this a lousy government, but I have concluded that it is not an adjective you would be willing to allow to be added to our Parliamentary vocabulary."

On American football:
"Actually it is somewhat like rugby. But why do you have all these committee meetings?"

"I would have liked to have been examined in history, poetry and writing essays. I should have liked to be asked what I knew. They always tried to ask what I did not know."

— *My Early Life*

"They [his school fellows at Harrow] all went on to learn Latin and Greek and splendid things like that. But I was taught English. We were considered such dunces that we could learn only English."

— *My Early Life*

A pharmaceutical company that specialized in condoms was commissioned to produce sheaths to protect the muzzles of British guns from temperature changes during the advance into Norway. Inspecting the first box of products to be delivered, Churchill muttered, "Won't do."

The next box he examined met with the same reaction, "Won't do."

A third box produced head shaking and more mutterings of "Won't do."

Finally, an aide asked what he meant. "They are long enough for the muzzles–10 and a half inches," the aide said.

"Labels," came Churchill's staccato reply.

"Labels?" his aide questioned.

"Yes. I want a label for every box, every carton, every packet, saying 'British. Size: Medium.' That will show the Nazis, if they ever recover one of them, who's the master race."

Questioned on whether he was aware of the British concerns on the Korean conflict, he responded:

"I am fully aware of the deep concern felt by the honourable member in many matters above his comprehension."

– 1952

Amid a lengthy, dull speech by an MP, Churchill spied an elderly member laboring to hear the commentary with an ear trumpet:

"Who is that fool, denying his natural advantages?"

Responding to a civil servant's critique of his use of sentences ending in prepositions in official documents:

"This is the sort of pedantry up with which I will not put."

"By being so long in the lowest form [at Harrow], I gained an immense advantage over the cleverer boys. I got into my bones the essential structure of the normal British sentence– which is a noble thing."

– *My Early Life*

In 1951 Churchill called for "a parley at the summit."
The word has since come to embody a high level diplomatic
meeting world over.

Coining the phrase "special relationships" in 1946:

"Would a special relationship between the United States and
the British Commonwealth be inconsistent with our
overriding loyalties to the World Organization [U.N.]?"

On appeasers:

"Each one hopes that if he feeds the crocodile enough,
the crocodile will eat him last."

– "The War Situation" speech, 1940

"The word 'disinflation' has been coined to avoid the
unpopular term 'deflation.' I suppose that presently when
'disinflation' also wins its bad name, the chancellor
(Sir Stafford Cripps) will call it 'non-undisinflation'
and will start again."

– House of Commons, 1949

Commenting on an MP's description that economic planning
was baloney:

"I should prefer to have an agreed definition of the meaning
of 'baloney' before I attempted to deal with such a topic."

– House of Commons, 1953

"You are afraid to eat your words; there is no need to be.
I have eaten a great many of mine in my time and on the
whole I have found them a most wholesome diet."

– *The Second World War, Volume. II*

On rejecting an academic career:

"I could not contemplate toiling [at Oxford in 1899] at Greek
irregular verbs after having commanded British
regular troops."

"Broadly speaking, short words are best, and the old words,
when short, are best of all."

– "Riches of English Language," 1949

"Let us be contented with what has happened to us and thankful for all we have been spared. Let us accept the natural order in which we move. Let us reconcile ourselves to the mysterious rhythm of our destinies, such as they must be in this world of space and time. Let us treasure our joys but not bewail our sorrows. The glory of light cannot exist without its shadows. Life is a whole, and good and ill must be accepted together. The journey has been enjoyable and well worth making–once."

– *Thoughts and Adventures*

BIBLIOGRAPHY

◆ ◆ ◆ ◆ ◆

A Biography of Edward March, by Christopher Hassall, ASIN: B00005X9B0.

Churchill, by His Contemporaries, by Charles Eade, Hutchinson, 1953, ASIN: B0006DAG1E.

Churchill: Taken from The Diaries of Lord Moran: The Struggle for Survival 1940-1965, by Charles McMoran Wilson Moran, Cherokee Publishing Co., 1976, ISBN: 0877971897.

Great Contemporaries, by Winston S. Churchill, Simon Publications, 2001, ISBN: 1931313709.

Marlborough, by Winston S. Churchill, University of Chicago Press, 2002, ISBN: 0226106330.

My African Journey, by Winston S. Churchill, Mandarin, 1990, ISBN: 0749301996.

My Early Life: A Roving Commission, by Winston S. Churchill, Pen and Sword, 1989, ISBN: 0850522579.

My Years with Churchill, by Norman McGowan, Souvenir Press, 1958, ASIN: B0006AVR2Y.

Painting as a Pastime, by Winston S. Churchill, Scribner, 1992, ISBN: 0684194538.

Portrait of Churchill, by Guy Eden, Hutchinson & Co. Ltd., 1945, ASIN: B0006D9SAE.

The Caged Lion: Winston Spencer Churchill 1932-1940, by William Raymond Manchester, Joseph, 1988, ISBN: 071813222X.

The Irrepressible Churchill, compiled by Kay Halle, Facts on File Publications, 1985. ISBN: 0-8150-1316-0.

The Proverbial Winston S. Churchill: An Index to Proverbs in the Works of Sir Winston Churchill, compiled by Wolfgang Mieder and George B. Bryan, Greenwood Press, 1995, ISBN: 0-313-29433-X.

The River War, by Winston S. Churchill, Wildside Press, 2002, ISBN: 1592249930.

The Sayings of Winston Churchill, edited by J.A. Sutcliffe, with an introduction by Robert Blake, Gerald Duckworth and Company Limited, 1992, ISBN: 0 7156 2389 3.

The Second World War, Volumes I-IV, by Winston S. Churchill, Mariner Books, 1986, ISBN: 039541685X.

The Story of the Malakand Field Force, by Winston S. Churchill, Barnes & Noble, 1983, ISBN: 1566191270.

The Wicked Wit of Winston Churchill, compiled by Dominque Enright, Michael O'Mara Books Limited, 2001, ISBN: 1-85479-529-5.

The Wit & Wisdom of Winston Churchill, James C. Humes, with a foreword by Richard M. Nixon, Harper Perennial, 1994, ISBN: 0-06-017035-2.

The World Crisis, by Winston S. Churchill, T. Butterworth, 1937, ASIN: B0006DLCZ8.

Thoughts and Adventures, by Winston S. Churchill, W.W. Norton & Co. Inc., 1991, ISBN: 0393029425.

W.S.C. A Cartoon Biography, compiled by Fred Urquhart, with a foreword by Harold Nicolson, Cassell & Company Ltd., 1955.

Winston Churchill: A Brief Life, by Piers Brendon, Secker & Warburg, 1984, ISBN: 0436068125.

Winston Churchill, An Intimate Portrait, by Violet Bonham Carter, Smithmark Publishers, 1995, ISBN: 0831758686.